MW00625975

Journeyman

to J.K.R. Yellowhouse

Journeyman

Stephen Thomas

Tsunami Inc.
WALLA WALLA WA 99362-0033

Copyright © 1997 by Stephen Thomas

All rights reserved. No part of this book may be reproduced or utilized in any form or by any means, electronic or mechanical, including photocopying, recording, or by any information storage or retrieval system, except for brief passages for reviewing purposes or in the fair use of creative pursuits, without permission in writing from the author or publisher. Direct requests for permission and orders to:

Tsunami Inc.

PO Box 100
WALLA WALLA WA 99362-0033
http://www.wwics.com/~tsunami
tsunami@wwics.com

Library of Congress Catalog Card Number:
97-60377

Thomas, Stephen
Journeyman / poetry
Selected Poems

ISBN 0-9644440-3-8

Cover design by Marie McCaffrey
from a woodcut by Jost Ammans, circa 1525

Printed in the United States of America

First Edition

The man who finds his homeland sweet is still a tender beginner; he to whom every soil is as his native one is already strong; but he is perfect to whom the entire world is as a foreign land.

Hugh of St. Victor

Acknowledgements

Some of the poems in this collection were previously published in *Exquisite Corpse*, *Contact Two*, *The Temple*, *Raven Chronicles*, *FishWrap*, *Point No Point*, *Ergo!*, *White Clouds Revue*, *The Malahat Review*, *Parallel Discourse*, *Art Access*, *The Seattle Times* and *Nobody's Orphan Child*. A substantial portion of them also appeared in the book *Venom*, published by Current, David Hiatt, publisher. The author would also like to thank Matt Kangas, Gary Adams, Marie McCaffrey, Patrick McRoberts, Charles Potts, Mark Svenvold, John Olson, Phoebe Bosche, Belle Randall, and Scott Preston.

other books by
Stephen Thomas

Confluence: A Portland Anthology
edited with Steve Dennison and Barbara LaMorticella,
Multnomah Arts Council, Multnomah 1979

Poems	Tomahawk Editions, Seattle	1981
Dichotomies and Holes	Reading Text, Seattle	1990
Venom	Current Press, Walla Walla	1991
The Sirens' Song	Red Sky Press, Seattle	1991
The Wheel	Basement Books, Seattle	1994

A Texan Jesuit Who Used To Play Left Field

The choices narrow down to these, he said.
You can perfect your art or self.

There are great fools,
failed men and women,
at the back of masterpieces,
cowards, bullies, drunks for whom love
is bent.

And saints are good for nothing.
They go up without a wisp of smoke.
They leave no ash, are rapt
in Godhead as the weather is in air.
Those whose names survive
were that much less.

Yet fate will not be fooled.
Serve one or serve the other.
Both you cannot serve.
Though neither is enough.
It's misery or disappearance.
Choose, he said, and fail.

Stiletto Heels

A rattler isn't poisoned by its meat.
Swallowing its kill whole is how it lives.

Maybe the first specimen of vertebrate with venom
had no stomach for it, died
digesting its first bite.

A little failure in the scheme.
We'll call it narcosaurus
for the sleep it now enjoys.

I made it up. Of course! So what?
The planet must have sired some such sometime.
Guesswork too can shed an honest light.

See then in the narcosaur's small failure
how the law succeeds. The planet
isn't hipdeep yet in oxymorons:
gophers freaking out in tunnels
acrophobic eagles, fish
that panic out of sight of land.

Go ahead. Relax, since logic rules
and rationalists thrive,
like women dressed to kill, but not survive.

At The Metropolitan

I wandered there into a sparse grove of marble,
where both ravished and appalled I gazed on the display:
dickless antiquities, nose- and earless, altogether headless,
limbless loped trunks out of Goya's widowed fancy.

In another room were columns topped with heads,
busts broken from their bodies by history's hammers
in our hands,
or executed by the portraitist,
guillotined in the conception,
also nose- and earless, lacking in the chin.

Is there yet another room where curators retreat to howl?
Where elbows, noses, earlobes, dicks, nipples,
all the protuberant detritus,
hangs arrayed in ghost postures,
like bits of fruit in aspic?

Time is a disdainful portraitist
and doesn't love us much.
It sculpts away the finished marble,
finding the shape within.

True to its grieved and solitary genius,
what it shows us is ourselves alright,
senseless and dismembered.

Venom

Plum petals drift in ugly masses
on my neighbor's concrete deck.
Three weeks loveliness half gone
to rot, and I despise him.

All our intercourse has curdled
like a failed sauce,
the *piece de resistance*
of a malicious dinner.

Both his bird-brained offspring,
evolution's darlings,
can distinguish Blass from Perry
Ellis at ten yards.

Let them perish, if it come to that.
They add no beauty to the afternoon.
The most they nourish is a few mosquitoes.

When I got wise to his disorder,
I was too sincere for buttered malice.
Point-blank I let him have it,

"Force a choice, I'm for the bees.
A dose of epinephrine
in a throwaway syringe
is all you need."

Fear is deaf to reason,
and it knows its rights.
It can outlive anything it chooses,
bees or species.

The prick,
he has a box of doses. Still
he cringes in his skin
as though it were a suit of dynamite.

tick tick tick
Destroy the clocks!
"A single sting can kill you.
So *tant pis*."

His look suggests I must be mad.
A feral swarm has no rights to protect.
How compare some insects to a man?

fearless
selfless
indispensable
indeed

The laws were his, of course.
My forced choice was to watch
a fat-wit pest technician come at noon
like a demented angel to my rented porch.

He hatched an apparatus from his truck,
closed his workday bible on the text
that reads "Work Liberates,"
and gassed the hive.

The Finest Turkish And Domestic

This tube you suck
like suicide
is not the tit of sister Death
but one of Power's thumbs.

She married him,
her first rebellion.
Now they live with you,
since Mom and Dad disowned her.

Do you need the rent? He beats her.
Up here in the attic,
your retreat,
you hear their savage partying.

They keep you up all night,
hammering duets out on your blood,
they and their guests, the Fears,
Mr. and Mrs., a pair of swingers.

You could go down and save her,
but, although you love her,
you would not embrace her.
And she your only sister!

Poem

I met the Buddha on the road.
I knew him by the light: it played
like music at his lips and eyes.
"Awakened one!" I cried.
He yawned.
"I do desire to be desireless."
"You'll get over it," he said.
I said, " I seek a quiet mind."
He said, "Shut up."
"No, really," I rejoined,
"I'll follow you wherever you may go."
He said, "I'm
going to go to sleep." And did.
He snored. I grew bored.
Persistent flies buzzed at my lips and eyes.
At last I cried,
"Buddha Schmuddha!
Enlighten my sweet ass."
He said,
"Now you're talkin."

The Wheel

1.
My daddy made me reinvent the wheel,
and this was every day. Yesterday's
invention never did. "That
just won't do," he'd say.

I did what I could
with parts and parts of parts,
with lefts and rights and
interchangeables,

until the theories and
abstractions fledged and
flew. I watched them,
half admiring and more than half

annoyed, resentful, staying
put, while all the little
yesterwheels, done and
abandoned, lay
beside their ruts beside the road.

2.

My daddy made me reinvent the wheel.
And I mean everyday.
Yesterday's invention never *did*.
"That just won't do," he'd say.

His own wheels, cartoon crude,
served well enough his ends,
but every day in darkness,
when we rose, he bumped me out

into the walking world. "O man,"
he'd say, the problems pressing in.
"Good God." It made him sad
to have to think.

I'd find the tools once more
on the wet lawn.
Their pale impressions stayed
where I had left them in the grass.

I'd set to work, and he would say,
"You give a man a fish,
three days and he'll curse you.
Teach him how to fish,

he'll curse himself."

3.
My daddy made me reinvent the wheel
out of darkness in the waking hour,
out of silence, articles of
light and sound, unpromising

materials, I thought, but
with the habit on me
strong almost as breathing
I made do.

And did I mention
it was unforgiving?
No. I see I didn't. Well,
perhaps it wasn't. Only

everyday to make it up,
whole cloth, seems harsh
from time to time, like
putting frozen fingers right to the fire.

4.
My daddy made me reinvent the wheel.
I don't mean lengths of logs;
the pyramids were up and running;
nothing crude fit in.

Not a tool mark marred the polished hubs.
The bearings in their raceways
whirred like smoke without
a click or tap or wobble.

Only tools with pedigrees were used,
their provenance traced in unbroken lines
to Lisbon and Spinoza, forged of carbon steel
as pure as Henry James' unsullied mind.

You see it wasn't just the drawing
board, not just conception
that the old man harped on,
not the *machina* that the *deus* used.

And not the baby pickled in the jar
of formalin. He wanted some
repeatability. "You show me how," he'd say.
"There is no *what* without it."

5.
My daddy made me reinvent the wheel.
I don't mean so to speak.
For him the fiction was the only thing.
The agony of parts inspired no pity in him.

How the tool steel screamed,
as it sank its tooth
into the hub block on the lathe,
the lathe which I'd invented more than once

and would again. The spoke wire
trembled like a martyr,
as I drew it out from the
extruder in the hissing workshop air.

But never, though the elements cried
out and the tools cried, never
did he say, "There. Make more of *that*.
That's what I call a wheel."

6.
My daddy made me reinvent the wheel.
and this was every day. Yesterday's
invention never did. I tried, of course,

and tried to steal the neighbors' wheels
or borrow even from my cross-town
enemies a little round, a caster

or jeweled movement. He
would catch me out. For
penance it was molecule by molecule from scratch, until

I'd had enough and swore
to be my own and own and Ouch!
it hurt each time I spoke

but spoke I did. I
had to. You
would too, if yours were mine.

7.
My daddy made me reinvent the wheel.
Year after year from darkness mixed
with light and unknown
substances, glimmers, notions,

feels. It was far more than he
could even start to understand-
or maybe just admit. I'd
got beyond his ken, the way

a son should do, I guess.
My wheels were not the kind of wheels
he grew to use and used to. But-
O, ever more important particle!

O, pivot of the universe!
which elsewise runs dead flat,
straight as a habit- But!
he let me go at last and him I let.

8.
My daddy had ideas and a disaffection.
"Wheels!" he hollered," Wheels!"
until the world grew dark
and distant and the turning,

unimaginably fast,
appeared almost as stillness.
All the wheels and all the wheels
within exploded, slowly, so it seemed.

I saw their milky ruts from under,
or above, and couldn't find
the sense of where I stood, until
the dark revolved. The sparks

flew from the [one remaining] dish and
hung. Then habit helped me out.
Dizziness went down, as I
bent, tasked, above my bench.

9.
At dawn each day and often
in the chill night at,
if I need add, my daddy's urging, I
would reinvent a wheel or so.

The moon spun on my finger,
gyroscopic, tilting,
holding against common sense
something of its own.

The spilled milk of the stars
gathered on my workbench
an assemblage of its own
pale peripheral parts.

10.
Daddy, I make wheels. It's what I do.
Wheels have become my be- and end-
almost. Were anyone like you to try stopping me now,
telling me, "That's enough! No more wheels now.

It's over." I'd say, "Who d'you think you are?"
And I would be afraid. Belligerence and fear
go rim and hub, arbor in spindle,
go in gone, round in around. But look!

There're *whee*ls and wh*eels*.
Whatever I put down comes up
and back. Around what goes around
comes. So: "Whatever," as Patty Borman's

father said and died. There's
nothing new, which means there's
nothing old beneath the sun,
of course, except the moon.

11.

When I awake, it's wheels, as
when I fell asleep, all
concerning wheels: their
reference, circumference and context,

wheels. And when an ambiguity
inheres, as when I say,
of him and me, "We'll tire
of this contraptioning

and folderol. We will
refrain from *tra-la-la*
one day. We will, I swear,
we will get off this wheel awhile,"

why then what
might and can and do
and ought and have and shall
I mean, but wheels, wheels.

Coriolis

This blue-green, turning globe
capped white and sleeved in cloud white,
racing in the sunlight on its wobbling plane,
among the swifter, slower, other-featured
miniature planets on their several ellipses,
draws the mind into its mobile envelope,
where a recurrent system of the middle
North Pacific shows one huge and fluid
gear, rotating opposite the clock as
it advances east and north and barges inland,
trailing skirts of squall. Across Pacific
County's logged-out hills, across Grays
Harbor where the cones of shake mills
and the Satsop towers pour their gray plumes upward,
move the weathers that will stall among
Olympic peaks, dump yards of rain into high valleys, or
shoved southward, roll and lower to the basin of
the Sound, where unobstructed they involve
sea level airs in their high passage, dragging
this among the inlets and the islands
over and around the West Seattle headland
to the traffic-studded bay, and inland more
to crowd among the cloud-capped towers,
peopled hills, across the Regrade and beneath,
confined inside the tunnel of Old
Ninety Nine at Battery and out and north,
the involuted sifting never ending in-between
the condos and the houses. How it slips

and pours above, around the four floor box
of Aaron's Ministorage, down the hill at
Crockett to be split upon the southwest
corner of the place next door and over
the garage to find an aperture high up
the wall and our small room.
It runs its sudden fingers up and
down the metal blinds below which
you lie in the striped light of the early
afternoon and over us and down the hallway
to the glass door, open on a single, tiny,
snowless peak and out to spill into the currents
ranging mountainward to pile up there and storm.

Weed Song

Colossal, astride a rocky pool,
  low among mussel encrusted blocks
          strewn at the base of Yaquina Head,
          where out of sight the Lighthouse squats,

I sheltered away from the constant wind
  and could barely make out the sound of surf.
          Surf disappeared in the ground of itself
          like the sound of my breath and sound

of my blood, the low, repetitive silent sounds
  against which fluctuations sing.

          Two brown weeds at the mouth of the pool
          anchored by rubbery webs of roots

drew my eye from the mussel shoals.
  I caught them taking a sudden wave
          and stretching inward, tips interspread,
          as they fanned poolwidth, a yard perhaps.

Influx struck at the rim of the pool
  and falling back drew pool water out
          which bowed the broad basal stalks of the weeds
          and pulled them currenting into the gap

till next wave struck with diminished force
  and drove them fanning out in again.
          Several turnings of ebb and flow
          established ebb as the dominant force.

Emerging swirls drew spread tips close,
narrowing into the gap at the roots
and towing them finally seaward out
to fan the shallows and musical stones

spreading out wide, a couple of yards,
before the course reversed again. I
squatted to watch as the weeds worked back,
mincing the force of stone-broken waves

till they spread again confined in the pool.
This was a small, particular song.
It drew me smallways into itself
with a local, mild sort
of slackwater pull
and held me entranced awhile
until
I pricked up my ears to a change in the sea.

Poem

Weeds jitter in the breeze out back
behind the Clinic
where ranters breach.

The crackhouse,
held together
by paint,
proves itself historical
according to
its own brass plaque.

I used to know a woman
hereabouts. I
see her sometimes yet
in memory's eye: hands
splayed flat on my chest,
she tosses blond hair back
and back. She groans.
She rocks.
She groans.

Where has she gotten to? Where
has she gone?
Where
has anyone gone? On.
On and on.

Coming home from work by dark

Coming home from work by dark
I think about the prospect of my place,
a high cold room in a condemned warehouse.

There I'll hug the oil-filled heater with my knees
beneath the desk and stay dressed in my sweater
and my coat until the kettle sighs.

Insists. Whistles. Shrieks
like a martyr surprised!
Then I'll make the tea.

I think, "It's always been like this,"
in Salish lowlands anyway
where winter weeds the old, the sickly and neglected out.

Of course, I know the legal set allows,
so long as I have money,
me to spend with all my fellows all the stuff of earth:

cordwood, coal, the lives of salmon runs,
oil and uranium:
because we're European.

Still that which I seek,
(fuel aeside) 's the same:
some heat to cook and live and sing by, of.

Carpenter's Son

Under the hood of the Ford in the doorless garage,
I aimed the flashlight; he taught me the terms:

The son-of-bitch.	The goddam son-of-a-bitch!
The bastard!	The fucking bastard!!

He taught me how to strip a bolt and
how to misplace wires. Of course, I
swore I'd never be like him:

freezing in the dark,
contemptuous, bored and scared.

It cost me forty years of busted knuckles,
echoing his terms, to learn
how to forgive, to learn to pay
a mechanic.

Two Photographs Imagined In The Garden

You have to be willing to go inward,
which of course is outward all the way.
If you stay here, where I found you,
with the pea vines and the skeletons of all
that used to live here, every hour of every
year will be sixty minutes of resistance
and no commercial interruptions.

The pea vines throw their supple grapples
everywhere. They are like us: when they
contact nothing, they embrace themselves
and collapse. The skeletons grow brittle and gather
a film of dust, which is history, breathing,
which is prehistory. So even if you choose
to stay here, pea vines and dusty skeletons
crook their fingers and draw you on a spidery
thread inside, where it is both the glum man
shirtless at the table stubbing his Pall Mall out
in his plate of eggs, while the glum invisible
woman captures him and all the rest in
black and white, which are gray, and
it is the both of them together, flowing
across the dance floor, he
masterful and she, she in a rapture of devotion.

The Rut Of The Mandala

I grew up in a round world, counting the days
to Christmas, Easter, birthdays, the Fourth of July.

Each year took forever, and I couldn't wait
or wade in my best boots through that much time.

I hoped I'd be surprised.

Until in middle age, like Christopher
Columbus, I discovered India, I thought.

The world! The world is flat, is linear. I
won't be sailing round it, gathering the prizes as I go.

Limited, whirling, strange,
a particle, colored and charmed, I

curled from an uncontrolled, but
willed collision into this molasses.

Measure my life in fragments. See me
hang fire here between Sweet Being and Has Been.

Wherever I head from here
is anybody's guess.

Poem

I suppose it had to happen.
All the things we must forgive ourselves:
the little murders in the house and garden;
a little luxury here, a misery there;
plenty, famine; God, the Almighty Bomb.

None of it ever really
the last straw. We've shrunken
Him down to a Puff of Gas,
a Thing so tenuous we can pretend
we didn't even know we did Him in.

It was ourselves we killed.
That's how it is with murder.
The suicide kills the world, the
murderer himself, but whoever
killed God, that
was a real Jonas Salk.

Fear Of Silence In The Catskills

The ground of being lies here at our feet,
falls away to bottomlands, Charlotte
Creek's evident meander, and past

the highway, New York 26, follows,
not quite streamlike, the generality
of the land's lay. Sexsmith Hill carries it
again skyward, closing the landview south.

For the moment New York City's cosmopolitan
miseries lie elsewhere. Here a high contrastive
silence rises. I imagine trout rising under the leaning
trees, snapping at flies, real flies, feather and steel
flies; raccoon dabbing crawdads in the shallows;
spider's killing among leaves. The world feeding.
I listen to its music is quite small.
The less I think the smaller it becomes
until I listen to a sound the shadows make,
a song of alignments.

Elsewhere I would wonder what the language
wants to mean. Here it is the land itself
I cannot fathom. I imagine huge
a whirring in the stars, which vibrates
through no medium except mathematics. Yet
it manages to coax the vole into the owl's view.

Here is a place where, since I must,
a man could live and die. Here I could hope
whatever fandance of electrons, salts and ions,
wherein moves the weave of feeling thought,
the origin of song, could settle in
to differ little from the silence, present as the wind...

Until the weekend neighbors rearrive from Yonkers.
Their's a stereo can broadblast Montevani polka
straight across the Sexsmith, right through
Rainbow Gardens in Butts Corner where
the country/western houseband also sounds
        real bad.
How small you are and frightened, says the noise.
I am your made brave face. Forget. Forget.

No Orpheus

The sense of self that occupies the mind
and clings to everything like down to grease
in imitation of a nest where cradles pain.
Molly-coddle in its tongue means goad.
Nourish means deny, to soothe to irritate.
Pain gets backward, putting on the brakes
it rushes nonetheless at what it hates.
And when it sings, it sings...and when it
sings, it is no Orpheus.

When that one played, the trees
plucked up their roots and danced the pavements
vigorous. Every animal exulted in its voice
When Orpheus got up, and every monster,
even Cerberus, grew mild as a retriever,
lapping its master's hand. The creatures
bopped in joy to his myxolodian tunes.
Even the stones shouted out.

                                        But when
the self I'm talking about starts it up
to sing, then you can bet the birds
drop dead as wood; the wood drops
dead as stone; the stone...the stone...
The stone just gets more stoned.

Poem

god was a girl you can't get
one you can never enter
try as you might
she's beyond you

god was a silken rag
you were a piece of amber
whatever you want to mean
you have to find god and rub

find her
you have to
find her
this the onliest option

one great truth remains
you could have had
any woman you only
had not to want her

James And Marilyn

They've done so much for us,
our living and our dying,
taken our risks and said
what we had to say but
were too timid to express. They've
murdered, rioted and traveled
back in time and forth
in time so many times,
as though
they could tame time
to our stalled will,
which also we gave over.

O, we gave so much
we envied them, their
perfect beauties as
their perfect lives. We
gave them the idea of
perfection, which
so overpowered
the complexities of their
small failures, even their
petty flaws grew large
and perfect and beyond us.

Kite our prayers, our crosses
papered with their images,
the knotted ragtails of our

curbed desires
to stabilize their fragile skyward urge.
We kneel before these stars.

They've gotten out of hand?
They've flown away?
The precious silver of them,
flattened out so many million
million times to gild our
little altars, televisions,
boudoirs, libidos and cars,
to decoupage our tea trays
and our dreams, returns
post holidays as litter
splayed at the fences' feet.

Jingle Bells

Chopping out the beat
with my three foot iron machete
on the holly stump,
I make a compost of
tomato shoots, hedge clippings,
gangly strands of ivy.
Come Christmas
it will be
one hot heap.

July 27, 1996

Sea Mind/Shore Mind

Sorting the same things over
again: hardware, lumber,
tools, parts: I find
new categories
new adhesions.
Shift. Sift. Drift.

Cattlepath Hollow

World is charged with event: light
on leaves shedding shadow on shadow;
songbirds burdened with song; insects
stupid with sex; each of us thinking
his thoughts.
                    When everything happens
at once, when order erupts, periodicity
fails, the mountain blows, trees fall,
dams burst and the song ceases.
                                        Still
the felled trees lie like spokes to the peak's
gone hub; ash rides high air currents
undisturbed; torrents rush downhill
to pool; so insects reappear and birds
return, while seeds take root, where angels
cannot dance, to reassert the victory
of weeds.
            Mostly currents bleed the pressures
off: tremors spend the force pent
in strained stone; a fat bee takes its weight
from a bent fern frond; a mayfly spawns;
thrush sings; you speak as a gold leaf
falls aslant within a slant beam of the sun.

The sun's replenishing rage is channeled
to a capillary's fineness for the small
exchange. Everywhere renewal.

Here in my heart that beats
are cells that loosen and fist.
Currents at place in flesh
course with viands and codes,
rubbing a protein's coils,
sustaining the heat that is me,
source of my voice and this song.

Here in this hollow we sit,
enclosed in a cellular shade,
our speech confused among leaves,
our boots in the hoofworked mud.
A leaf rides the shitfouled stream
and is ignorant of the sun.

Love Poem

Now I have dulled ten pencils
twice and
can't improve upon *I love you.*

Words so dull and rusted with abuse
I didn't think could take and hold an edge,

until I honed them to your name.

They became quite keen enough to cut.
What I mistook for rust on them
is what becomes of blood.

Garage Sale

Gulls, crows, raccoons
come to mind,
as to a garbage can.

The omnivores and
opportunists,
brethren:
like the muledeer
with the washboard ribs
nuzzling through the horse shit
for an oat.

Everything comes
to mind, if
only to be dismissed.

Sure the mainframe seizes; debt
washes Iowa south
as a hundred channels fizz.

But long before we bust the concrete slabs
to free the convicted farms,
we wring these rags once more
of a few sad drops of home.

Perspectival

Everything was different
when I remember:
Taller, farther, stranger,
more to be desired.
everything hurt worse
and lasted longer:
high up in the tree
time was more like oil,
less like gasoline.

Except for falling. That's
the opposite. What
used to be a blurred green rush
goes now
more slowly, is
viscouser, more
eventful.

Rivermoon

I didn’t need to imagine it full.
The moon hung off to my left above
Marquam Bridge and round as the mouth
of a jar. It drew me out from myself
into the chilly space where its white light
stilled the brilliance of near stars.
Still it wasn’t the moon hung full in the sky
so much that caught my eye and brought me
to a stop along the rail, as down below
the liquid rivermoon, gone silly on the channel
near the dike. A lambent motley moon of
five, six lobes, playing it loose with
borrowed light relent from the dark river.
Not figured moon but more a quicksilvery
play and interplay which scientific thought
might analyze to superficial curves, incident angles
and weld again in heat of mind with
mathematic flux into a disc. Just beautiful,
stupid lobes. I looked my fill
and pedaled on. The full moon hung and spun
above the bridge, while down below that other
spread on wind-worked shallows wide
into a sheet of water-sparks. I stopped
again to look and asked, What do I make of this?
There was the actual moon hung full in my eyes
and there a field of stipplings on dark water.

Oh, it was moon all right. Yes. it was moon-
light, all the broken notes of a full,
round chord, gone falsely elemental
like a drunk on the strong dark drink
of the river. What in the world is a moon,
I wondered, that should go so wild on river water?
Came no answer and I made for home.

Lakemoon

I hung one wish
which was weightless
from Arcturus
where it shone
in a monster
whale's tail
pigform
bust of Descartes
making west while
I waited for transport east

noticed moon
how to put it
made out
moon
pale mottled berry
beer barrel big
poisonous bolus
bright brown round
risen

lake couldn't
swallow
but stretched that
elastic lozenge

into a crazy pile
of plates
gyrating
fluid edged
almost electric

call it a goddess
call it *sum ergo*
call it an invitation

moon my enormous
desire for darkness
moon my unsmiling
need of denial

moon axis
volatile light
oh virgin
soiled and unsteady

moon my moon
and only two million
watching

A View From Iowa

facilis descensus Averni
noctes atque dies patet ianua Ditis
set revocare gradum superasque evadere ad auras
*hoc opus hic labor est** —Virgil

And I would have left that country there and then,
since knowing they had little that I wanted
or could use, I had grown wearing looking for an excuse.
What kept me there? Why was it I had come?

The Dodge stood at the hilltop, parked
among some shrubs in a cul-de-sac,
an easy climb traverse the steep slope
where a few stones stood in hollows
scooped out from the hill. At least
we'd had no trouble getting down,
except to keep our footing.
Someone had maintained the graveled path,
trimmed the borders, plucked out every weed.
They may perhaps have salted down the ground
along the way. Below us where the incline
gentled out a yard, surrounded
by a harrowed field and wire fence,
contained some upright stones and fallow lawn.
Above us on the flat a close grave crowd
of listing, weathered stones stood aging,
mute, among the shadows of enormous elms,
which stood the summit ground for all I saw
the compass round.

Something in the dead, the locals say,
on which they feed, keeps lightening off
those trees. And since they stood unblasted,
shapely, tall, I could as well believe it was
the dead as chance or grave-ground elves
or prayer kept devastation off them.
Chance is not a theory I embrace in all
its numbing implications. Elves, if there are elves,
you never see. And as for Christian prayer,
I recollect it never seemed to sway a cause for me.

Phyllis was for going from the place.
She had the creeps. The sun was going down.
The sky above us, starless still, was blank,
as empty as a salmon tabled eye.
Around us an horizon-distant bank of towering clouds
stood dark and looming, brilliant in the west
with gold, vermilion, violet and green.
There we stood alone among the stones
of an Iowan boneyard, Phyllis and myself.

I'd come, I guess, since Phyllis was my girl
and it was Easter week, an empty time.
I'd hitch-hiked west from Michigan,
while she by train crossed mountains,
rivers, plains from just outside Spokane
to this small town of Woodbine, where her father
kept a farm. Her parents set me up in the hotel
and fed me meals and hoped I'd marry Phyll.
I'd come, I guess, intent on laying off
the burden of my shy virginity,
if that's the word.
I'd come to find my heaven upon earth.

I realized too soon, the second night,
that Phyllis knew the laws of measuring
her favors. So far only, not below the waist.
I was nineteen, disgusted by her lack of grace.
I suffered her to let me kiss and tongue
her upper half above the scar of birth,
and that was that. No coaxing, pleading,
anger or blind thrust would make her yield.
It wasn't love. It wouldn't last forever.
Well I knew. It didn't last the week.

And there we were, my last night
in the heartlands where the corn had just been planted
that would feed the nation's foredoomed cattle.
The wide Missouri lay off in the west,
invisible, as were the plains beyond.
A hundred Melvilles, Auburns, Battle Creeks
were picturable there between our cemetery hill
and what I missed and always thought I'd see
from the next rise, mountains! snowcapped,
ponderous, barren, beautiful limits of sight!
Phyllis hung and pled upon my arm.
She wheedled, made rash promises and tugged.
The sun sank down into the bank of clouds,
while something held me there to witness dusk.

A light leapt out. A rift broke in the clouds.
Everything went russet all at once.
And I was deeply rooted to the spot,
while Phyllis fled. I heard her footpads
running up the slope, the car door open, slam,
the engine start, the gravel spray.
She didn't wait -I have to hand her that-
but left me there among the quiet stones
to watch the vision with the sunlight fade.

The stones especially returned the light.
A pale red glow as though they warmed within.
The elms above and all the grass green slope
took on the hue of fevered, waning life.
And that was all. The rift closed in the clouds.
The stones went blank. The elms became a tangle
once again of darker darkness on a darkened sky.
A nameless brilliant star or two appeared
among the boughs, like winter fruit.
I made my way back slowly up the hill
and at the summit caught the warlike flash
of silent lightening storming from the east
and closing in.

*The road to hell is smooth, an easy ride,
and day and night the doors stand open wide.
But to retrace one's path to air that breathes,
That's a scramble over rough terrain.

Labyrinth

This is my domestic monster:
minatory brow with horns,
a flaring snout and rust red, matted hide.
He's bellowing like New Year's gone askew.
Aw, he's so fake and silly,
rented bull's head, moulage scars and all.
Just bad Hollywood fantasy,
B grade horror stuff
to scarify a misbehaving child.
I'd tear his mask away, but when I reach,
my finger tips touch finger tips like mine.
We're two arms' lengths apart,
my homey terror and myself.

This is my amazing home:
these endless halls, blind stairs
and nowhere doors that open on my hoards
of nothing. I should know them well;
they're my design.
But I have lost my master plan and lost
my old familiar spider
which I'd learned to trust.
I'd use her thread to follow my way out.
My monster must have eaten her.
He feeds. He feeds a very little, but
he feeds. I cannot starve him out
from my confusing house.

And now for my confirmed confusion this:
under his fake brow and wooden horns,
where eyeholes cut to fit his eyes should show
the red eyes of an imitation bull,
are real eyes, white lids and human lashes.
Wild! I am the frightened child.
Tears whelm in his eyes for sorry fear.
The lashes flutter as I lift my hands
to my own face and tear. My monster
likewise paws away his mask. We stare.
His face unmasked is mine and in his eyes
I see reflected his bull's head on me.
Then monstrous knowledge dawns and he takes wing.

To See A Life

Sirens screaming, and
it has begun.
Before you know it
's in your blood,
quick as a struck match
flares. Fire? Crime?
Or Heart Attack?
Or Holocaust? It's there.
Emergency. You're
anyone. A crawling
scalp, a pulse
caught in a throat.

Until,
as red trucks roll,
incongruously slow,
into view,
annoyance reasserts
the self. I
turn to see
a dark plume
risen in the air above
the lakeside road
where I just passed
five minutes back.

It's natural,
my curiosity.

The shattered day
assembles once again

around this new
emotion,
fire eagerness.
Bright medallions,
orange, yellow, red,
defining lines of sight
I did not know existed
in the dense, enormous laurels,
rhododendrons and
bare alders of the hillside.

There a bower opens,
concrete stairway
rising in the dark.
Blind to traffic,
I am drawn across
the roadway, upward
two steps at a stride, until
I'm there:
                    a little, unkempt lawn,
a little stucco house
with white walls
vertical behind
untroubled shrubs.
Blown windows
pouring sheets of flame
into smoking eaves.
An open porch door,
roaring like a demigod,
forbidden by a temple
veil of flame.

Firemen unrolling coils
of flattened canvas hose,
shouting, hustling, taking
their positions and
ignoring
one fat man in shirt sleeves,
shocked and ineffectual,
who demands that things
be saved, *The Records!*
All the Records!
At his feet behind
a heap of smoking
rags upon the flagstones.
What he must have
rescued as he fled.
Odd what panic saves.

How very like a temple
that place, where
the sacredness that holds
aloof in things
erupts! I might think
that the laws
of physics acted there alone
as they had to act, except
there's order in the law.
And nothing can explain
this roaring change:
how what is ordinary
can contain
what I found there:
Possessions, furniture,
bedding, books & records,
circuits, cabinets, rugs, lathe,

clothing, ornaments, walls
all fuel to flame. Every-
thing the man in shirt sleeves
had amassed to put
between himself and cold
& darkness had just
turned him out and
embraced itself. What
he had saved, those
rags to which my awed eyes
turned for rest, had better
have been left to show
forth what he had to learn
of god before he learned
of love, the power and
indifference. The firemen's hoses
filled and flexed. They
braced themselves and aimed
the stangs into the flames.
A hissing joined the roar.
Terrified, I saw
the rag heap stir.
The world exploded
once again
to rearrange itself
around a man: the black
skin blistered, flayed,
streaked red, a trace
of muscle, blistered
cranium, no hair, hands
fingering the dirt.
Then at his legs
a senseless metal trellis
suddenly made sense.

His walker. How
he must have shuffled
in his flames out of
that door and pitched
off of the porch three feet
to come to himself there
bleeding, dying
on the flagstones and the dirt
behind a leafless rosebush
on his homeless lawn,
as the house roared
what he alone perhaps
could understand.

I laid my jacket
helplessly across
his skinless back,
and summoning at last
a stretcher for him
(no one had seen him and
no wonder that),
took the jacket back.
At last I recognized
a character to me well-known,
a crippled bachelor,
as short of temper
as of breath and so near
death my only wish for
him was that his animal
heart would seize and
free him.
I prayed
let him die and let
them burn him.

Let some flame designed
for changing flesh to ash
consume the rest of him,
complete what has begun
beneath the open sky.
What else but
sensibility could save so
hard a death.
Failing that fail all:
there is no resurrection then
except as smoke ascends
against the sun and the
prevailing/winds disperse the pall.

The Existential Railroad Lyric

Hey, pretty mama, I'm a railroad train.
I choose and choose and choose.
I got a means a locomotion I just can't explain.
It's choose and choose and choose.

I used to think I was a carnivore.
I preyed and preyed and preyed.
But it cost too much and I just got bored,
as I paid and paid and paid.

So now, pretty mama, I'm a railroad train.
I get to pick my tracks from here to Maine.
I might just cross on over to Spain,
if I choose, if I choose, if I choose.

So stoke my engines and turn me loose.
I got champagne on ice in my blue caboose.
And you can come on along if you like the refrain,
if you choose, if you choose, if you choose.

Discontent

As he lay once in sweat and love's contentment
next his sleeping lover on a Sunday noon,
he felt a brief touch at his shoulder, turned
his admiring gaze from her he loved
and saw the curtain rise on a humid breeze.

A pallid moon
hung full above
the heat hazed land.

A glacial valley
cut in distant hills
diminished in the haze.

I don't know what it meant: spent he lay there next her,
while his mind in discontent spoiled for adventure.

The Power of Negative Thinking

Wish what is away, because
if you can, it will go, rocketing,
almost echoless, following
phlogiston, Anaximander,
Ectopistis migratorius, Bohr's atom
into forever's preterit box,
bigger than all the moon.

Now you see the slate renewed,
the smeared residuum of unrecoverable marks.
So we remember dreams that disappear in us,
troubled, little recalling, less.

Now imagine what the chances are
you will be wanting another go round,
have any use for tender,
legal or funeral, need
further assurance.

Once we were asked to entertain the sequel's question.
Has the anniversary passed of my demise or
is it still to come this winter?
Will I care who lives me out?
What of these remains,
when I'm past choosing,
of my oath and will?

Ah, but you will live forever,
pale as the comfort,
still as these pages,
hearing what you cannot listen to
and trembling like a web, untenanted,
still white with dew.

Flightpaths

The hazel's coppery tangle
where the catkins hang in rain
comes briefly into life
with red-crowned kinglets,
tits in bandit masks,
a solitary jay.

All nerves and twitter,
cautions and crakes,
they move about the open brush
like thoughts in idle brains.

Neighborhoods I think
are tired of
our big ideas:
families, orders,
classes, kingdoms.

It's not that *thinking*
was a bad idea.
It was never an idea,
but it closes on itself
and revs.

Our gardens
will make weeds of us
when there are
no more *weeds*
or categories.

Maybe it's just me but
in the jets' approach
I hear the roar of war.

Concentration

Lars Thorsen's big-boned son stalked into the paddock,
if you call it stalking.
He walked right in, chambering a cartridge as he walked.
He didn't mind being seen.
From twenty feet he drew a level bead on the young beef,
but the thing spooked and bounced off lively through the
 clumpy grass
to where it settled down and grazed again.

Lars Thorsen's big-boned son didn't get impatient.
He circled at an even pace around the paddock,
till he raised the "twenny-two" again.
The Hereford liked this game.
He leapt and gamboled off again.
He bounded through the thistle and then strolled,
you could call it strolling, underneath the tree of
 unripe apples,
out into some new grass where he settled down at last.

Lars Thorsen's son came round,
more slowly this time,
through the waist high strawgrass,
till he got round to the brow end of the beef.
He knew what he was doing.
The Hereford's young companion was sequestered in the barn.
The steer looked up at Thorsen's son through puddle eyes,
registered no interest and fell to cropping grass.

The gun went up. The Hereford raised his head.
There was a pop, like a lady finger, and
the steer stood still an instant, trembling maybe.
Then it went down forelegs first in the grass.

Lars Thorsen had been jawing at the paddock gate.
He spat and climbed into his truck.
The little rancher threw the gate back.
Lars drove in on a rutty track,
arced into the high grass and backed up till his tailgate
must have been about above the fallen carcass.
I went back to work.

Twenty minutes. They had everything inside.
A yardarm, block and tackle swung out back.
They strung it up, beheaded, skinned and gutted it.
Out came heart and lung tree in their slippery colors.
Liver, kidneys, stomachs, tripes and glands.
Everything about went up into the truck.
They hauled it off and didn't close the gate.

I made my way out to the matted grass,
fascinated by the speed and change.
All I found where it had gone down were two
heaps of green manure and several brilliant
smears of blood, equally covered with flies.
They were serious, those flies. I swatted at them with
my broom. They wouldn't budge.

Turning Compost

So much to have unlearned in learning
to love this sweet, rich, septic reek.

The passages retraced.
The codes cracked and abandoned.

Steams rise from torn layers of black rot,
a stink like dung, enough

to make me gag until
I think my way around the reflex. Soil

in the making. Humus. Soon
Comestibles. Then man. That's me, the one

who drives the tines into the layered pile,
like Schlemann's Troy, but here the treasure

gleams otherwise. I unearth and rebuild
both at once, pitching leafmold, chopped

stalks one bin to the next. I am
the pile's lungs. Breath is labor. As I

pause, panting, leaning on my pitchfork's
haft, I see myself in a new light:

How the dull pile seethes. It seemed
as simple as an empty sky, as

passive as the moon. But it's
alive, aswirl. Each gouge shows a raging

life: worms flex and coil, beetles
scuttle, centipedes entrain among the crumbs

of steaming earth and torn mycelia.
I stand to wipe the sweat out

of my eyes and see, high in the poplar's crown,
the alabaster clouds, the bitten moon.

Plum(b)

The plum tree at my window
fingers the dark breeze,
while its companion shrub,
an arborvitae, quivers
as if with intent.

Out in the night spirits move.
In here beneath electric light
my hands alone across
an auditorium of keys.

What is this mind of mine
that pesters plants, molests
the weeded lawn with
reference? It senses itself
sensing and is sad.

I do not know. No,
I do not. Inside
there are no pivot points, no
exit lights, no absolutes.

I'd let the mute plants
grow out there and idle cats
stalk thicket birds un-
interrupted, but
there's something still I'm
itching to express.

Where will I find the force or grace
to leap the gap, to bridge the drop
into these bright phenomena,
these dark events?

Something in the mind
that wobbles with desire,
if it were let hang, if
all the skittishness had
settled out, and it
were to hang true,
so looking on itself
forget itself and
look upon the plum,
if that were so...

What else were there to do?

Deconstructing Bedford Falls

Language is like Jimmy Stewart, if
you take my meaning: see him
play the stay-at-home who
feels the itch but never
gets away. He's lost
that sense of self that comes of being
hero in the hero's tale.

Duty ate him up and shat him out:
the Building and Loan, old Potter's Bank,
the Town, the Crash, the War.
See property is theft, the theft of self:
my house, my job, my mind, my hands, my feet.
What's left for me to be behind this matrix of possession?
My birth. My Life. My death. My my.

Trust Heaven! How it
intercedes as Hollywood
to see our hero home,
who's us.

It gets complex, this sleight of screen:
George found the crack in being:
that's imagination:
slipped into an absence:
stepped beyond the cave:
from which Platonic lookout:
the abode of unborn souls:

he framed life as never after so unhappily:
Being is a wink like an electron:
Nowhere is our other home for Now.

Aaaand
there's less:
from nowhere comes your paradox.
It lets our Jimmy/George desire what he possesses,
need what he doesn't lack.
Satiety just whets his appetite.
Sick of home he's homesick still in town.

Your language does that:
puts your absence all around your heart,
pictures continuity in blinks, like calculus,
where continuity *an sich* would be a blur,
and, telling its own story,
lets you catch my drift.

Now, here's the word from Hollywood.
Kids, don't try this at home.
Leave it to Jimmy Stewart.
He knows what he's doing.

A Man Walks Into A Bar

A man walks into a bar.
A man walks into a tavern, into a lounge, a pub,
        his kitchen, the cellar.
A man walks into a fight, a porn store, an affair.
A man walks into a bar.

He slouches, skulks, sleepwalks, rushes, stumbles,
        dives, crawls into a bar.
A man who has tightened his tether and now is
        drawing it short, coiling it round the spool
        of a bottle, a thought, his penis, an ego
walks into a bar.

A man or a woman, a boy or a girl, a child walks into a bar.
A man who is sick of his manhood, for whom to be man
        is only a burden he breaks his back in denying,
a woman who is sick of womanhood, for whom to be woman
        is a burden she breaks her back in denying,
a child walks into a bar.

A boy or a girl, arrested in some first awareness,
awakens again at a bar stool, a porn booth,
        a fist fight, a rented bed.
A boy and a girl, two boys, two girls, a boy and his dog,
        a girl and her pony are locked in an embrace
        without understanding.

A man walks into a bar.
He has himself in his wallet.
Spend all he can he cannot find or lose it.
Spend all his juice he cannot touch another.
Spend herself senseless she cannot touch.
Drink herself stupid she cannot.

A man walks into a bar.
In the aqueous half-light of the smoky mirror
what appears to him, sipping at history,
shattered among the glasses?
What does he see?

He sees *me*.

The Devil To Pay In The Backlands

Darkness fell with rain this evening,
pattering at glass in dusklight as I
slowly came awake. I listened as
I'd listened just an hour before
and peered between the screen slat
at the robins tugging earth worms from
the green, wet lawn and drifted
off to sleep. I lay alone
upon the wide, hard bed, the book
I had been reading on my chest,
a long, hypnotic monologue
delivered by a man who must have lied,
and yet it was all fiction, love and
magic, urgent, opulent until
I sank loose-minded into fitful
sleep and colored dreams of flight,
dispute and further flight, dissolving
in the moment of my waking into growing
darkness and the sound of rain.
A flight of starlings
raveled from the holly, plunged into the cedar,
disappeared. The rain asserted its chill,
dappled hiss, and laying back
I read the sullen gray intensifying
dusk against the dark graph
of the bamboo screen. When something from the dream
or book came forward in the mind to raise

a voice of warning or regret and I
began almost to speak...But there
was no one to address. The birds had
gone, while I remained with this,
a husk of thought, just one recorded
fact, that in this quiet place
this evening darkness fell with rain.

Syllables

for Ruth Jenny Davis

She'd no more memory in her
than has a wheat field
and what she meant repeating
why why why
didn't seem a question

not because she didn't pause
to hear an answer

How do you answer the wind
in the cedars
How do you answer the stream
where it pours over stone

Maybe she got too old and
should have died before she
lost what we call sense

That was how her children
comforted their grief
repeating *This is better*
This is better

But I prefer to think
that Earth which in its range
is still less old than she
is singing to the sun

a song of gratitude and pain
and that our syllables
beyond what we intend
are joined in that long song
the music of this sphere

her eyes are blind as the moon
her ears deaf as the sea
her lips are stopped with earth
the field round her grave has been sown

No Shade

for E. Clyde Davis

Why should I wonder
I wonder
what are the facts
when granddad recollects

Memory doesn't lie
so much as reinvent
the way a painter reinvents
a truth which passive eyes
could not extract
even from a nest of facts

Liars of course
however much they call
upon the actual
cannot portray beyond
convenience anything
like truth

Why then should I wonder about facts
unless his fictive truth
strikes too near home
when granddad speaks

He's folded on the couch
his bony knees up level with his chest
He coughs and laughs

and tells me in those days
outside of Cushing, Oklahoma
it was pretty near a hunderd in the shade
and adds
No shade

They keep the parlor warm for his old bones
and for the bones that sit across the room
the woman he calls she whom he ignores
as I try to ignore her aimless speech
her vacant cloudy eyes

She does not recognize
this man with whom she lives
and has lived since before the war to end all wars
and while he speaks from memory to me
he looks at her with bright and lashless eyes

My Father's Garden

Father is no visionary. He,
although the planets all align and
comets flare dangerously near,
will lie asleep upon his winter couch
and, waking, rise to kneel to his nightly prayer.

Heaven opens once and only once
for such as he, who, salt and seasoned
of the tended earth, condone no fantasy.
His hands are hard with use and his addictions
grim. He senses fitness in the bone
of suffering, and he believes in sin.

Once in his garden father, through my eyes,
was asked to make acquaintance of a mole.
He did not pause or even seem to feel
the hand of Monster Chance
that brought the creature crawling to the pit
where, dazed, it tumbled into daylight.

Mocking something, I began to speak,
O, Gentle Spirit... Father struck
with accurate quick hoe
the animal in half. My
tongue was cleft.

Though heaven open wide in spring to show
the frightening, swift trippets, cogs and belts
of star machines, the blinding brilliance
if the father god, the several and sever-
able hearts of damp earth worms,
or any dissimilar thing, father,
unsusceptible to these, will bend
to lace his boots and, rising, go
out to his garden shed to fetch his tools
and ply their blunted edges in the soil.

Garden Song

for John McManus

Darlings, this is Eden where the worm
rooms with us, spending Sabbaths home
to dine on fruit
that does not care if it will ever ripen
for the self-protecting rose.

Darlings, this is Eden where the lion,
full of heart, lies down next the lamb,
and lamb arises
in the lion's flesh to graze no more
on the green sweet grass in life's sweet fever.

Darlings, this is Eden where we dream
to find our blessings mixed with shame.
While cool moons pour
bright pools in the dull gutter,
heart beats tattoos to its only end.

Darlings, this is Eden whole and all,
and no appeal will elevate the soul
to any other.
Here the dawn's damp streets are paved with gold,
and evening's banners on the bare wall shudder.

The Poet At 41

In this skinned nose and these small eyes
is something that he wants to take
in metaphor for all the world.

Is this because I've always sat
in front for some dark window, my only model,
with dozens of neighborhoods, several cities,
glimmering through his glazed brittle skin?

Tonight another rented room and all the blinds are drawn.
It is the traffic sounds from 99 and from above,
the ramps of air into the jetport south,
that make these thoughts resemble a backlit scrim.

We're each in this alone is the first thought.
Our dark doubles tell us so is two.
And moving down the ramps of air comes three:
alone is all that binds us, all we have in common, all.

Asking Directions

*Truth is...*he shouted and nearly didn't
go on. An oddity of current caught
at his raft and spun it round a spindle
tether in and in and in until
it stood neither still nor progressing but
held and revolved. The wobbling forenoon sun
struck into out of into his eyes as
the axis transfixed him, amazed, from the
crown of his head through his vitals and groin
the raft and river and river bed to the core
the earth. He was stalled.

                                                            The weeds went giddy.
A pair of gabbling mergansers atilt ducked and
were gone. I had joined him, reeled in on the spools
of our sight, empathic and dizzy with pity and
terror, until my gorge rose and I cried like
Ulysses tied to his mast. When a drift log struck
and he sat down hard as the eddy released
him. Holding his head in his hand he
continued *Truth is you keep to the path you're on.*
Dizzy I leaned on a cottonwood, waiting.

Summer

I had been waiting so long for summer
that, when it arrived, my momentum
kept the mercury down. The very
dogs huddled near fireless stoves,
and flowers closed to the bees, just
like a girl I knew in Iowa,
O, thirty years ago.

Meditation At Lake Union

I.
I left you in a rich and unconfined confusion,
wandered down this hillside to this lake,
sat down beneath this tree, unquiet oak,
and thought about interior restraints.
How each leaf of this oak divides the wind
and, rising, makes to fly . Come fall they will.
But these are rooted through the lashing twigs
and twitching branches, swaying boughs and moving
limbs to upright trunk which stands its ground
to ground, while Eddie, whom you know and seem
to like, sits on the deck below and watches
ships. Unquiet shade! I wander among
voices, stoned on acid, wishing I had
a white hat, swift horse, six-guns
and a worthy cause or two or just a sibyl
who could penetrate this noise of oak,
this rasping rush of foliate confusion;
hear and rescue from this tissue clash
god's or fate's or nature's bell-clear word.
I wonder at desire's form and motion.

II.
We're headed for the gasworks whose machines
stand rusted, rigid, motionless and gaunt.
We talk about the edges of seen things,
how levels of abstraction meet and rub:
water at the shoreline, light on leaves,
the world, whatever is the case, *der Fall*.
I wonder what the language wants to mean.
I wonder what you're waiting for and whom.
I might say, You are waiting for a man
without cuirass, greaves or helmet, free
of impediment whose entire flesh is his
Achilles' heel, someone wielding Ockham's
razor with a deft hand, willful and uncluttered
with a mind like Praxiteles'.

III.

One sees in even such a puddle as this lake
the curvature of earth. The water bows
and, glancing silver, seems about to swallow
up the gray, top-heavy town. A ketch
out on the water fills its sails, which, bellied
taut, upon the masts pull. Eddie tells me,
headway is the thing. Sailing's just a matter
of full sails. The air attenuates
to slip in streams around the perfect shape.
A partial vacuum draws the vessel on.
I wonder where it is you want to go.
I can imagine women under broad-brimmed bonnets
sitting in the sun on a verandah, glancing out
to sea to right and left of the blind bar
shrinking to meet the low sun, sipping
iced drinks, gossiping like fates,
filling hours with pleasure, seeming not
to wait, although their eyes may linger
on the line of sea and sky.

IV.
Eddie and I discuss love's definition:
stealing kisses across the asymptote.
I am inclined to redefine the whole,
eros, *thanatos*, fate's geometries,
toss out the parallel infinitudes, planispheres,
the whole marvelous, abstract machinery,
the entire metaphysical gasworks,
learn to sail a ketch and set a course
for St. Croix or the isle where Circe dwells,
to contemplate the sea, chockfull of clouds,
the ribs of sea wrecks and the setting sun.
I wonder what is your desire's form and motion.
I envision shrouds of being filled by steady
needs. They shape themselves in parabolic curves
to fit whatever wind will serve to keep them
bellied taut and motionless and pulling at
the pliant, upright, central, simple fact
of creaturehood, to draw you onward toward
some meeting place or some commercial pier,
whatever, through a partial vacuum.

The Sirens’ Song

Call me Ulysses. Call me Prince of Guile,
master of more tricks and turns than Ptolemy.
There isn't much I stick at. Little disgusts me.
Most things I'll try twice.
Tales I have to tell
of Troy and of the sea of the Middle World,
tales you know already of the things I've been and done:
a war resister, faking madness at the plough,
a diplomat and breeder of wooden horses.
I've fucked witches, made old Proteus cry Uncle!
mocked the monster Polyphemus,
after I put out his only eye.
Derision long outlasts the pain of wounds.

And I have been among the gray dead,
asking questions, prying into things.
I've learned what I don't mind telling,
even if few believe, and it makes me mad.
The gods have set us up where we are proud,
like pins, and they compete to knock us down.

Things I could tell you make a strong man sick:
Circe's tricks, her cowardice, her harlotry,
and she a goddess in eternal bliss;
the snapping sound of human thigh bone breaking
between teeth
among shrieks wherein pain and horror compete;
how war weary soldiers in the face of victory
kill everything that's enemy, even furniture,
cradle and wheelchair, in the grip of pure blood glee.
Ordinary soldiers, I tell you. Ordinary men.

I've also heard it said my wife of twenty years,
though only a year's bride the day I left,
kept company with no man in my absence.
Her name's become the watchword of fidelity.

Listen:
Anybody tells you that a woman in her prime,
who has offers and likes sex,
spends twenty years, the only life she has
without so much as a hand gets in her pants...
Don't marry the teller's daughter.
Don't let him sell you a boat.
His head is full of something, and it isn't facts.
There's something on his mind experience can't dislodge.
It has nothing to do with women or with boats.

Penelope is clear eyed, and she knows her station.
Queens cannot just fuck and walk.
Anyone lays a queen, anyone, that is, who is her equal,
doesn't want to be her equal but her lord.
That's how it is with property:
the more a woman has the more she's seen as such.
It wasn't her companionship her suitor's wanted.
It was oblivion.
They thought a king need never be himself.
They thought their gnawing emptiness could be
evaded by command.
They thought and proved the value of their thinking.
What they knew...They knew nothing.
Now they groan in hell.

Penelope should be the word for perspicacity.
She saw what her suitors wanted.
Not a strong willed, handsome woman with dark eyes,
equally eager to laugh and to lay.
Not an equal. Not a wife.
They wanted Ithaca, a stage for posturing.
They wanted to strike fear in other hearts
to eclipse the fear in their own.

I've been among the exhausted dead. I know.
I have authority which neither badge nor office can augment.
Doubt me if you will;
I've heard the Sirens sing.

The tale is plausible, I think, like all my tales.
Believe who will. It goes like this:

When we returned from Hades and Persephone's cortege,
Circe entertained us on the beach,
the men with wine, myself with anecdotes of the immortals.
The bonhomie among the crew gave place to brags,
the brags to brawls, the brawls to bonhomie,
until at last like children angry with fatigue,
their bickering subsided into sleep.
Then I, who shared the goddess's bed,
kept watch beneath the circling stars,
while Circe set to fill my heart with fear.
She planted images in mind, what lay ahead,
the Sirens, rocks and maelstroms,
monstrous presences and holy cattle,
the commonplace encounters of a hero's youth.

Point by point she laid out every danger, every choice,
enjoying, as I saw, in her imagination
    my prospective horror.
And she warned me not to venture into earshot
    of those fishy witches called the Sirens,
who would see me dead of false promises
    and pretty noise.
Knowing me as well she might, considering my long,
    bewitched sojourn there on her island,
she knew that I would have to hear what had destroyed
    my kind before.
She knew I would insist as children will on having
    what must harm me.

And she told me how to bring it off.
Everybody knows the story nowadays:
how I informed Perimedes and Eurylokhos what to do
once I had stopped their ears:
to bind me to the mast
and, when I struggled, double up the bonds.

I asked myself...I should, that is, have asked myself
why Circe would assist in this.
Why would a goddess in immortal bliss,
who owed me nothing in the scheme of things,
reveal this trick to me?

Strange humors move the gods.
To ask their motives is to interrogate the wind.
We sail among their wills.
And all our mastery of seacraft
is the knowing of the limits of ourselves and of our boats.
We choose at their direction.
Their will will be done.

Soon after dawn we sailed.
I told my men enough, not everything of course,
lest desire and fear make mutineers of them.
I led them to believe I had no choice
except to listen to the Sirens' song.
And so, of course, I could not choose but choose.
I stopped their ears with kneaded beeswax,
and then I had them tie me to the mast.

I got to know that mast, its rough spots
and its smooth, its degree of taper,
how it widened downward,
tightening my bonds when I relaxed.

And what occurred?
I stood awhile
against the mast anticipating,
like a young man at his wedding, when his bride
in silks casts long and knowing looks upon him.
Everything illicit in her father's house
will, in some hours, be allowed.

The oarbeats measured time, like spoons of honey,
    slowly, slowly out.
Longing and uncertainty together stretched
awareness taut. And time stood for a time
completely still. Repeated oarbeats seemed
the one beat caught in an endless, undiminishing
echo. Noon it was and summer solstice.
Thirty-seven twenty North by twenty-seven East,
The zenith and the nadir of my years.

Sweet music came across the glass green sea.
An open candid air in harmony
One clear soprano and a husky alto,
redolent of sex, the kinds of voice
that draw me like an insect to a lamp.
The tune was such I heard it in my belly and my groin.
My scrotum tightened and my sex got hard.
Delirium took hold of me from inside,
like a hunger or strong wine, and I was overcome.

As often as I've told the tale,
I never would admit until this moment
that the words I heard were vivid as a dream and
dreamlike disappeared except for a nagging trace.
I think they offered endless willingness,
vigorous invention, pure transparency.

Everybody knows how married love has its opaque corners,
where unfathomable otherness is lodged.
The best intentions of a hero's will meet this and quail.
No force of arm or mind can make it yield.
It is the man in the woman, the woman in the man,
the other other in the spouse who breathes against all will.
The Sirens' song dismissed opacity, promising
compliance, telepathy, pussy as pretty
as the crease in a just ripe peach.
Everything a man knew how to ask for,
more than he could know to ask.
All that was needed was a leap of faith.

The ribs of shipwrecks stood around that coast,
like pickets of a French fence. The beach
was littered with the putrid carcasses of seamen,
as the banks of spawning streams are
    littered with still salmon.
The stench was overpowering, the sight sickening.
Yet the Sirens seemed to sing to me that this
was an illusion, just a test of courage.
If I could dismiss the evidence of my senses,
I would possess their beauties always,
live always in their sexual embrace,
coming in great spasms, like the Nile at flood
fucking the very sea.
I wanted to believe them. And I did believe.
I looked upon that horrorshow.
I saw how empty were their images,
shadowy hags tricked out for midnight show,
beckoning from under awnings, under tawdry wigs,
distance and desire coloring what nearness would
    rinse blank.

Even while I knew their vacancy, I cried out,
    "Let me free!"
I wanted what they promised,
the shallows, the variety, and the lies.
My stomach rose into my chest.
My heart throbbed in my throat.
My head spun round as if with wine and smoke.
By god, my sex had swollen huge,
as huge as wild Achilles in his battle dress,
as huge as Troy in flames, as huge as Ithaca,
as huge as Greece herself.

Perimedes and Eurylokhos arose from their
    opposing benches, pinching at their noses,
    doubled up my bonds and went back to their rowing.
The oarsmen altogether gazed astern,
their eyes averted from that horrific shore.
Then the song grew visual.
It erased the picketed wrecks,
covered the corpse littered shore.
The stink itself transmuted from the rottenness of meat
to the sweetly salted ammonia scents
    of a woman's wetted sex.
The singers came to me as blondes and redheads,
statuesque black priestesses with full red lips,
brunettes in all attires and none,
beauties of all statures and complexions,
manners and desires,
full heaving breasts and parted thighs.

They were all beauty, all desire, all willing,
all in all in all and I could not get free.
The fetters cut my wrists.
Splinters worked their way into my back.
My tongue was dry and swollen and my lips were cracked.

Even so I might have spent myself before all eyes,
if we had not pulled slowly out beyond their voices' length.
Then, as the vision faded and I felt my age,
I heard among the dying notes a lonely cry,
as if my mother, Antikleia, bowed with age,
were keening for her father, Autolykos,
were keening for her lost youth, beauty, life,
wantonly recalling bouts of sex, and
angry with me, as with all my gender,
for our crimes and for the crimes of fate.
I shuddered then, as if I were King Oedipus
recognizing in his aging wife his aged mother.

And the singing died.
I was exhausted, sore and thirsty.
I had seen and heard too much
and even so felt my desire untutored,
for I hearkened back again to the Sirens' visual song.
Yes, I had more to learn.

I caught Eurylokhos' eye
and mouthed the words "Release me."
He gestured to Perimedes, who rose.
Then looking over me, he shook his head.
The mother of a willful child who hurts
himself and in a rage denies his hurt,
transforms his pain to anger and, once-burned,
determines he will teach the fire a lesson,
the mother of such a child casts such a look
as did Perimedes on me, before
he drew another loop across my chest,
cinched it up tight and went back to his bench.

Then I began to learn about desire.
I heard my heart above the oarbeats.
I felt the life in me those heartbeats
made and measured.
How it ran away.
How rapidly I fled through time,
like wine out of a torn skin,
like blood out of a deep wound.
My hands were numb.
A fiery, small pain developed
underneath my shoulder blades.
Time moved in two contrary rhythms,
rapidly toward death, slowly on toward evening,
when at last the sundown broke the spell that
held my oarsmen to their clockwork task,
and they rose to untie me, but not to set me free.

Shadow Madness

I measured my light in the sun.
How small it seemed.
Sun at my back I built my fire.
My shadow fell upon it.
I stoked my fire until I could not stand near.
My shadow fell before me.
Between me and my fire.
I have built my fire at night.
The cool moon mocked me.
Now I will burn this city.
I will burn my body with it.
I will burn them to the ground.
The sun itself will not find their shadows.

In Tranquillity

What is abundance
that a man should breathe
words above a page?
a woman breathe words

(remembering/foretelling)

the fall of blown rose petals,
brown around the edges,
in the first late summer rain?

Or any other sad phenomenon?
Or gay? Or

sitting on parole from romance
at a kitchen table
overlooking the electric lake
does a man or must a woman
seek the same excitement
felt in the attested heat
in this last act caught by the evening light?

Whose tenderness belongs in verse?
Or anyone's?
What nerves lie in the pen
or in the levers that intend
within this dirty manual
that feel as I feel now
or have remembered feeling?
And do they reach our wordward?
all the way?

Today

Today I am singing death because
I have to.
I am celebrating the insurmountable
loss in the face of which
everyone has cowered.

Today I am saying goodbye again
to the one and to the many,
to John and to the unremembered others
under their dated stones.

Today I'm sitting still to write this down.
I am pausing on the way from
          there to there.
At the wheel of my truck in the dark
I am counting, figuring, feeling...
with a red pen
-it came to hand-
on yellow paper.

Today I am reaching forward and reaching back
from John, who taught me love and thinking,
to you who have other purposes, other worries.

Maybe you have come to this with a sick headache
or after seafood with greasy lips and fingers
have cleared this strewage from a chair
where you intend only to sit and to digest.

Your intentions have been complicated.
Something's caught your eye.
The figure of the open book, face down,
a tent or hieroglyph, a glance, a word and now
the rest:
how Robert Schumann, dead at forty-six,
has reached across the radio to me,
mixed with my memories of John and
passed to you. One hundred forty years
from him to me, ten thousand million accidents
but one intent.

Halflife

Half my life in disbelief, because
I knew the world would fail in a blind fire
before any end found me,
I called my wars the world's,
since I was all there was.

I despised the ceremonial boneyards,
the paved lawns, the tasteless statuary,
permanent flowers, funerary rouge and
pale etiquette, chalk marks on the void.

Half my life in faith
I thought at least my self sense warrants
my dismissal of this nullifying race,
this greedy species, than which I am better,
worthier of godlove, more endowed.

Yes, I desired a name to place,
if I could find the place,
above a pair of dates and a terse
phrase like that of Yeats
or the laconic warriors of Thermopylae.

Now it seems it will outlast me.
Triumph will befall the undertakers.
Weeks and months rush whistling by my ears.
My wars are the world's wars certainly.
My denials are the world's denials, for
the world's are mine. The worlds are me.

Something out there's fattening this calf.
Real time is a measure of decay.

Ptolemy's Maze

I want to make you see
this ruin, innocence,
how it makes a hash of best intentions.
Watch the leaves fall from the sapling aspen.
I want to make you sense
the force of speech that darts and lances
through a fog of dread.
Put your open hand to my parted lips.
I tell you that I need to make you feel
conversion roll
like something out of Euclid,
striking so conspicuously true
in the reasoning mind
as to drown doubt:
        laws of mind
        and of brute fact
        run parallel and true
        as twin rails laid
        and staked to the rising roadbed
Hear that freighted moan.
Look here, sweetheart.
Nobody sets the world straight.
Each thing turns and turns.
A single stone, held pivotal in mind,
throws twist in nested twist
into the stars that it surround.

The scheme of motions of the local moon
in her epicyclic spiraling yearly career
swung round this long galactic arm
that hurtles out of bang into collapse
would appear on paper
as the doodles of a disturbed mind.

Don’t let it trouble you.
Forget the spider.
Look at the web.

Poem

I might as well imagine
as go out.
I have seen the residual light
freed of its skyward urge
crash to earth,
and images out of my dreams
hatch in the actual light:
fire astir in water,
water astir in air,
air astir in burrows,
burrows on fire-
slow fire locked in a blind crawler.

If I went out,
what could I hope?

In here it is warm,
and the songs come
from the timid birds.
Lumps of all elements
lay on the table,
slip in the molds,
playthings, pastimes,
amusement.
No, I needn't go out.

When the light fails,
the small ones will come.
Discarding their wings in season,
they play in approachable flame,
my guttering candle.

Inaugural Verses

The celebration of a change and of renewal,
differing visions, a persisting view,
has brought us here. The words we use
to speak of these important matters
are imported, carried here from other
continents. That these imported words
took root beside our rivers, which have names
as old at least as Britain, if not Rome,
Susquehanna, Mississippi, Yukon, proves
their vigor. Still we understand their limitations
in ourselves and in our history: the proclamation
of the rights of man by men who kept their slaves
and women in their places; pioneers displacing
native cultures from their paths. This is our past
in part and has to be forgiven, not
because that blind self-centeredness was innocent.
The past cannot be passed until unearthed,
          examined and forgiven.
Looking to the present, what we see is land,
the soil, the air, the water, infinite
gradations of environment and creatures
interwoven in seamless web of life, the ground
of all our values. If this great metaphor,
the land of freedom, is to live, if words
will carry meaning from the past, this earth
must mean as much to us as liberty.
Our true home may lie elsewhere;
the road is at our feet.

Stars

i.
The deeper night
they burn the brightlier.

On what is not themselves
they shed no light.

Of nothing they show more
more clearly

as among them stand
the parchments dark and emptinesses.

ii.
Here's where fancy paints
his most cerebral tales.

> highways of spilled milk
> unicycling animals
> ursine ladles
> fishless scales

Sky is not a picture
mind can otherwise hold.

Sky is piercing nonsense,
arrows, spear points, blades.

iii.
How we enter outward
balancing envy's beam,
the gymnasium of desire.

Naked, we dream of standing
alone where there's nothing to breathe.

Bio

Born in Auburn, Washinton in 1950, the last of six children of Elizabeth and Ernest Thomas (a bookkeeper and a carpenter), Stephen Thomas took the commonest route of escape from the Catholic working class: he left home at 14 to study for the priesthood. After four years of training at the defunct St. Edward's Seminary, he turned to the Jesuits at Marquette University where he completed his bachelor's degree with highest honors. He went on to study medievel literature at Cornell University. Again taking a common route, he escaped the anxieties of academic life by taking up his father's trade, which he practiced sporadically until 1993, when he took up the trade of teaching. He currently teaches at Cornish College of the Arts, University Preparatory Academy and the University of Washington Extension. He serves as Poetry Editor of *Point No Point*: A Blue Moon Reader. He is also a member of the steering committee of The Poetry Circus, an annual festival of spoken word in Seattle.

Photo of Stephen Thomas by Elliott Bronstein

Colophon

Journeyman
was printed during the Spring of 1997
by Thomson-Shore in Dexter, Michigan,
for Tsunami Inc. of Walla Walla, Washington.
The text is set in Times New Roman
and printed on 60# Glat Supple Opaque
Recycled natural paper.

Tsunami Inc.

booklist

Michael Finley

Lucky You	Litmus Inc.	1976	$5

d.a. levy

Collected Poems	Druid Books	1976	$10

Charles Potts

100 Years In Idaho			$10
How the South Finally Won the Civil War and Controls the Political Future of the United States			$29
Loading Las Vegas	Current	1991	$10
The Dictatorship of the Environment	Druid Books	1991	$10
The Opium Must Go Thru	Litmus Inc.	1976	$5

Signed limited edition numbered hardback copies of

The Dictatorship of the Environment	$30
The Opium Must Go Thru (hand quarter bound in leather)	$50

Teri Zipf

Outside the School of Theology	$10

Coming soon from Tsunami:

Pacific Northwestern Spiritual Poetry

an anthology 30 years in the making, edited by **Charles Potts**

Prices include bookpost and handling. Mail check or money order for the amount of each book to Tsunami Inc., PO BOX 100, WALLA WALLA, WA 99362-0033. View our books on the Internet at http://www.wwics.com/~tsunami and email for discounts and feedback to tsunami@wwics.com.